To:

_____

From:

_____

Date:

_____

"Be strong and courageous!
For the LORD your God is with you wherever you go."

JOSH. 1:9

He made us, and we are His. We are His people, the sheep of His pasture.

Ps. 100:3

Give your burdens to the LORD, and He will take care of you.

Ps. 55:22

Let God transform you into a new person by changing the way you think.

Rom. 12:2

"Anything is possible if a person believes."

Mark 9:23

I can do everything through Christ, who gives me strength.

"Blessed are those who trust in the LORD and have made the LORD their hope and confidence."

JER. 17:7

The Lord leads with unfailing love and faithfulness
all who keep His covenant and obey His demands.

Ps. 25:10

"Come to Me, all of you who are weary and carry heavy burdens,
and I will give you rest."

Matt. 11:28

"Do not be afraid or discouraged,
for the Lord will personally go ahead of you."

Deut. 31:8

Those who live in the shelter of the Most High will find rest
in the shadow of the Almighty.

Ps. 91:1

"I will never fail you. I will never abandon you."
HEB. 13:5

Kind words are like honey – sweet to the soul and healthy for the body.

"The joy of the Lord is your strength!"

Neh. 8:10

This is the day the LORD has made.
We will rejoice and be glad in it.

Ps. 118:24

Those who trust in the LORD will find new strength.
They will soar high on wings like eagles.

Isa. 40:31

"No eye has seen, no ear has heard, and no mind has imagined
what God has prepared for those who love Him."

1 Cor. 2:9

I will rejoice in the LORD! I will be joyful in the God of my salvation!

HAB. 3:18

Nothing in all creation will ever be able to separate us from the love of God.

My health may fail, and my spirit may grow weak, but God remains
the strength of my heart; He is mine forever.

Ps. 73:26

See how very much our Father loves us, for He calls us
His children, and that is what we are!

1 JOHN 3:1

"Blessed are all who hear the word of God
and put it into practice."

Luke 11:28

The LORD is my light and my salvation –
so why should I be afraid?

"Be strong and courageous!
For the LORD your God is with you wherever you go."

JOSH. 1:9

He made us, and we are His. We are His people, the sheep of His pasture.

Ps. 100:3

Give your burdens to the Lord, and He will take care of you.

Let God transform you into a new person by changing the way you think.

"God blesses those who work for peace,
for they will be called the children of God."

MATT. 5:9

"Anything is possible if a person believes."

MARK 9:23

I can do everything through Christ, who gives me strength.

"Blessed are those who trust in the Lord and have made
the Lord their hope and confidence."

Jer. 17:7

The LORD leads with unfailing love and faithfulness
all who keep His covenant and obey His demands.

Ps. 25:10

"Come to Me, all of you who are weary and carry heavy burdens,
and I will give you rest."

MATT. 11:28

"Do not be afraid or discouraged,
for the Lord will personally go ahead of you."

Deut. 31:8

Those who live in the shelter of the Most High will find rest
in the shadow of the Almighty.

Ps. 91:1

"I will never fail you. I will never abandon you."

Kind words are like honey – sweet to the soul and healthy for the body.

PROV. 16:24

This is the day the LORD has made.
We will rejoice and be glad in it.

Ps. 118:24

Those who trust in the LORD will find new strength.
They will soar high on wings like eagles.

ISA. 40:31

"No eye has seen, no ear has heard, and no mind has imagined
what God has prepared for those who love Him."

1 COR. 2:9

I will rejoice in the Lord! I will be joyful in the God of my salvation!

Nothing in all creation will ever be able to separate us from the love of God.

Rom. 8:39

My health may fail, and my spirit may grow weak, but God remains
the strength of my heart; He is mine forever.

Ps. 73:26

See how very much our Father loves us, for He calls us
His children, and that is what we are!

1 JOHN 3:1

"Blessed are all who hear the word of God
and put it into practice."

The LORD is my light and my salvation –
so why should I be afraid?

Ps. 27:1

"Be strong and courageous!
For the LORD your God is with you wherever you go."

JOSH. 1:9

He made us, and we are His. We are His people, the sheep of His pasture.

Ps. 100:3

Give your burdens to the LORD, and He will take care of you.
Ps. 55:22

Let God transform you into a new person by changing the way you think.

"God blesses those who work for peace,
for they will be called the children of God."

MATT. 5:9

"Anything is possible if a person believes."

I can do everything through Christ, who gives me strength.

"Blessed are those who trust in the LORD and have made
the LORD their hope and confidence."

JER. 17:7

The Lord leads with unfailing love and faithfulness
all who keep His covenant and obey His demands.

Ps. 25:10

"Come to Me, all of you who are weary and carry heavy burdens,
and I will give you rest."

MATT. 11:28

"Do not be afraid or discouraged,
for the LORD will personally go ahead of you."

DEUT. 31:8

Those who live in the shelter of the Most High will find rest
in the shadow of the Almighty.

Ps. 91:1

"I will never fail you. I will never abandon you."

Kind words are like honey – sweet to the soul and healthy for the body.

"The joy of the LORD is your strength!"

NEH. 8:10

This is the day the LORD has made.
We will rejoice and be glad in it.

Ps. 118:24

Those who trust in the Lord will find new strength.
They will soar high on wings like eagles.

Isa. 40:31

"No eye has seen, no ear has heard, and no mind has imagined
what God has prepared for those who love Him."

1 Cor. 2:9

I will rejoice in the LORD! I will be joyful in the God of my salvation!

Nothing in all creation will ever be able to separate us from the love of God.

My health may fail, and my spirit may grow weak, but God remains
the strength of my heart; He is mine forever.

Ps. 73:26

See how very much our Father loves us, for He calls us
His children, and that is what we are!

The Lord is my light and my salvation –
so why should I be afraid?

"Be strong and courageous!
For the Lᴏʀᴅ your God is with you wherever you go."

Jᴏsʜ. 1:9

He made us, and we are His. We are His people, the sheep of His pasture.

Ps. 100:3

Give your burdens to the LORD, and He will take care of you.

Let God transform you into a new person by changing the way you think.

"God blesses those who work for peace,
for they will be called the children of God."

MATT. 5:9

"Anything is possible if a person believes."

I can do everything through Christ, who gives me strength.

"Blessed are those who trust in the LORD and have made
the LORD their hope and confidence."

JER. 17:7

The Lord leads with unfailing love and faithfulness
all who keep His covenant and obey His demands.

Ps. 25:10

"Come to Me, all of you who are weary and carry heavy burdens,
and I will give you rest."

Matt. 11:28

"Do not be afraid or discouraged,
for the Lord will personally go ahead of you."

Deut. 31:8

Those who live in the shelter of the Most High will find rest
in the shadow of the Almighty.

Ps. 91:1

"I will never fail you. I will never abandon you."

Kind words are like honey – sweet to the soul and healthy for the body.

"The joy of the LORD is your strength!"

NEH. 8:10

This is the day the Lord has made.
We will rejoice and be glad in it.

Ps. 118:24

Those who trust in the LORD will find new strength.
They will soar high on wings like eagles.

Isa. 40:31

"No eye has seen, no ear has heard, and no mind has imagined
what God has prepared for those who love Him."

1 Cor. 2:9

I will rejoice in the LORD! I will be joyful in the God of my salvation!

HAB. 3:18

Nothing in all creation will ever be able to separate us from the love of God.

My health may fail, and my spirit may grow weak, but God remains
the strength of my heart; He is mine forever.

Ps. 73:26

See how very much our Father loves us, for He calls us
His children, and that is what we are!

1 John 3:1

"Blessed are all who hear the word of God
and put it into practice."

LUKE 11:28

The Lord is my light and my salvation –
so why should I be afraid?

Ps. 27:1

"Be strong and courageous!
For the LORD your God is with you wherever you go."

JOSH. 1:9

He made us, and we are His. We are His people, the sheep of His pasture.

Ps. 100:3

Give your burdens to the Lord, and He will take care of you.

Ps. 55:22

Let God transform you into a new person by changing the way you think.

"God blesses those who work for peace,
for they will be called the children of God."

_____

"Anything is possible if a person believes."

I can do everything through Christ, who gives me strength.

PHIL. 4:13

"Blessed are those who trust in the Lᴏʀᴅ and have made
the Lᴏʀᴅ their hope and confidence."

Jᴇʀ. 17:7

The LORD leads with unfailing love and faithfulness
all who keep His covenant and obey His demands.

Ps. 25:10

"Come to Me, all of you who are weary and carry heavy burdens, and I will give you rest."

MATT. 11:28

"Do not be afraid or discouraged,
for the Lord will personally go ahead of you."

Deut. 31:8

Those who live in the shelter of the Most High will find rest
in the shadow of the Almighty.

Ps. 91:1

"I will never fail you. I will never abandon you."

HEB. 13:5

Kind words are like honey – sweet to the soul and healthy for the body.

PROV. 16:24

"The joy of the LORD is your strength!"

NEH. 8:10

This is the day the LORD has made.
We will rejoice and be glad in it.

Ps. 118:24

Those who trust in the Lord will find new strength.
They will soar high on wings like eagles.

Isa. 40:31

"No eye has seen, no ear has heard, and no mind has imagined
what God has prepared for those who love Him."

1 Cor. 2:9

I will rejoice in the Lord! I will be joyful in the God of my salvation!

Nothing in all creation will ever be able to separate us from the love of God.

My health may fail, and my spirit may grow weak, but God remains
the strength of my heart; He is mine forever.

See how very much our Father loves us, for He calls us
His children, and that is what we are!

1 JOHN 3:1

"Blessed are all who hear the word of God
and put it into practice."

LUKE 11:28

The LORD is my light and my salvation –
so why should I be afraid?

Ps. 27:1

"Be strong and courageous!
For the Lord your God is with you wherever you go."

Josh. 1:9

He made us, and we are His. We are His people, the sheep of His pasture.

Ps. 100:3

Give your burdens to the LORD, and He will take care of you.

Let God transform you into a new person by changing the way you think.

"God blesses those who work for peace,
for they will be called the children of God."

Matt. 5:9

"Anything is possible if a person believes."

I can do everything through Christ, who gives me strength.

PHIL. 4:13

"Blessed are those who trust in the LORD and have made
the LORD their hope and confidence."

JER. 17:7

The LORD leads with unfailing love and faithfulness
all who keep His covenant and obey His demands.

Ps. 25:10

"Come to Me, all of you who are weary and carry heavy burdens,
and I will give you rest."

Matt. 11:28

"Do not be afraid or discouraged,
for the LORD will personally go ahead of you."

DEUT. 31:8

Those who live in the shelter of the Most High will find rest
in the shadow of the Almighty.

Ps. 91:1

"I will never fail you. I will never abandon you."

HEB. 13:5

Kind words are like honey – sweet to the soul and healthy for the body.

Prov. 16:24

"The joy of the Lord is your strength!"

Neh. 8:10

_____

This is the day the LORD has made.
We will rejoice and be glad in it.
Ps. 118:24

Those who trust in the LORD will find new strength.
They will soar high on wings like eagles.

"No eye has seen, no ear has heard, and no mind has imagined
what God has prepared for those who love Him."

1 Cor. 2:9

I will rejoice in the LORD! I will be joyful in the God of my salvation!

HAB. 3:18

Nothing in all creation will ever be able to separate us from the love of God.

My health may fail, and my spirit may grow weak, but God remains
the strength of my heart; He is mine forever.

Ps. 73:26

See how very much our Father loves us, for He calls us
His children, and that is what we are!
1 John 3:1

"Blessed are all who hear the word of God
and put it into practice."

Luke 11:28

The Lord is my light and my salvation –
so why should I be afraid?

Ps. 27:1

"Be strong and courageous!
For the LORD your God is with you wherever you go."

JOSH. 1:9

He made us, and we are His. We are His people, the sheep of His pasture.

Ps. 100:3

Give your burdens to the Lord, and He will take care of you.

Ps. 55:22

Let God transform you into a new person by changing the way you think.

"God blesses those who work for peace,
for they will be called the children of God."

MATT. 5:9

"Anything is possible if a person believes."

I can do everything through Christ, who gives me strength.

PHIL. 4:13

"Blessed are those who trust in the Lord and have made
the Lord their hope and confidence."

Jer. 17:7

The Lᴏʀᴅ leads with unfailing love and faithfulness
all who keep His covenant and obey His demands.

Ps. 25:10

"Come to Me, all of you who are weary and carry heavy burdens,
and I will give you rest."

MATT. 11:28

"Do not be afraid or discouraged,
for the LORD will personally go ahead of you."

DEUT. 31:8

Those who live in the shelter of the Most High will find rest
in the shadow of the Almighty.

Ps. 91:1

"I will never fail you. I will never abandon you."

Heb. 13:5

Kind words are like honey – sweet to the soul and healthy for the body.

PROV. 16:24

"The joy of the LORD is your strength!"
NEH. 8:10

This is the day the LORD has made.
We will rejoice and be glad in it.

Ps. 118:24

Those who trust in the LORD will find new strength.
They will soar high on wings like eagles.

Isa. 40:31

"No eye has seen, no ear has heard, and no mind has imagined
what God has prepared for those who love Him."

1 Cor. 2:9

I will rejoice in the LORD! I will be joyful in the God of my salvation!

HAB. 3:18

Nothing in all creation will ever be able to separate us from the love of God.

My health may fail, and my spirit may grow weak, but God remains
the strength of my heart; He is mine forever.

Ps. 73:26

See how very much our Father loves us, for He calls us
His children, and that is what we are!

1 John 3:1

"Blessed are all who hear the word of God
and put it into practice."

Luke 11:28

The Lord is my light and my salvation –
so why should I be afraid?

Ps. 27:1

"Be strong and courageous!
For the LORD your God is with you wherever you go."

JOSH. 1:9

He made us, and we are His. We are His people, the sheep of His pasture.

Give your burdens to the LORD, and He will take care of you.

Ps. 55:22

Let God transform you into a new person by changing the way you think.

"God blesses those who work for peace,
for they will be called the children of God."

MATT. 5:9

"Anything is possible if a person believes."

MARK 9:23

I can do everything through Christ, who gives me strength.

"Blessed are those who trust in the LORD and have made
the LORD their hope and confidence."

JER. 17:7

The LORD leads with unfailing love and faithfulness
all who keep His covenant and obey His demands.

Ps. 25:10

"Come to Me, all of you who are weary and carry heavy burdens,
and I will give you rest."

Matt. 11:28

"Do not be afraid or discouraged,
for the LORD will personally go ahead of you."

Deut. 31:8

Those who live in the shelter of the Most High will find rest
in the shadow of the Almighty.

Ps. 91:1

"I will never fail you. I will never abandon you."

Kind words are like honey – sweet to the soul and healthy for the body.

"The joy of the LORD is your strength!"
NEH. 8:10

This is the day the LORD has made.
We will rejoice and be glad in it.

Ps. 118:24

Those who trust in the LORD will find new strength.
They will soar high on wings like eagles.

Isa. 40:31

"No eye has seen, no ear has heard, and no mind has imagined
what God has prepared for those who love Him."

1 Cor. 2:9

I will rejoice in the LORD! I will be joyful in the God of my salvation!

HAB. 3:18

Nothing in all creation will ever be able to separate us from the love of God.

Rom. 8:39

My health may fail, and my spirit may grow weak, but God remains
the strength of my heart; He is mine forever.

Ps. 73:26

See how very much our Father loves us, for He calls us
His children, and that is what we are!

1 JOHN 3:1

"Blessed are all who hear the word of God
and put it into practice."

Luke 11:28

The LORD is my light and my salvation –
so why should I be afraid?

Ps. 27:1

"Be strong and courageous!
For the Lord your God is with you wherever you go."

Josh. 1:9

He made us, and we are His. We are His people, the sheep of His pasture.

Ps. 100:3

Give your burdens to the Lord, and He will take care of you.

Ps. 55:22

Let God transform you into a new person by changing the way you think.

"God blesses those who work for peace,
for they will be called the children of God."

"Anything is possible if a person believes."

I can do everything through Christ, who gives me strength.

"Blessed are those who trust in the LORD and have made
the LORD their hope and confidence."

JER. 17:7

The LORD leads with unfailing love and faithfulness
all who keep His covenant and obey His demands.
Ps. 25:10

"Come to Me, all of you who are weary and carry heavy burdens,
and I will give you rest."

"Do not be afraid or discouraged,
for the Lord will personally go ahead of you."

Deut. 31:8

Those who live in the shelter of the Most High will find rest
in the shadow of the Almighty.

Ps. 91:1

Kind words are like honey – sweet to the soul and healthy for the body.

Prov. 16:24

"The joy of the Lord is your strength!"

Neh. 8:10

This is the day the Lord has made.
We will rejoice and be glad in it.
Ps. 118:24

Those who trust in the Lord will find new strength.
They will soar high on wings like eagles.

Isa. 40:31

"No eye has seen, no ear has heard, and no mind has imagined
what God has prepared for those who love Him."

1 Cor. 2:9

I will rejoice in the Lord! I will be joyful in the God of my salvation!

Hab. 3:18

Nothing in all creation will ever be able to separate us from the love of God.

Rom. 8:39

My health may fail, and my spirit may grow weak, but God remains
the strength of my heart; He is mine forever.

Ps. 73:26

See how very much our Father loves us, for He calls us
His children, and that is what we are!

1 John 3:1

> "Blessed are all who hear the word of God
> and put it into practice."
>
> Luke 11:28

The LORD is my light and my salvation –
so why should I be afraid?

Ps. 27:1

"Be strong and courageous!
For the Lord your God is with you wherever you go."

Josh. 1:9

He made us, and we are His. We are His people, the sheep of His pasture.

Ps. 100:3

Give your burdens to the LORD, and He will take care of you.

Ps. 55:22

Let God transform you into a new person by changing the way you think.
ROM. 12:2

"God blesses those who work for peace,
for they will be called the children of God."

MATT. 5:9

"Anything is possible if a person believes."

MARK 9:23

I can do everything through Christ, who gives me strength.

PHIL. 4:13

"Blessed are those who trust in the LORD and have made
the LORD their hope and confidence."

JER. 17:7

The LORD leads with unfailing love and faithfulness
all who keep His covenant and obey His demands.

Ps. 25:10

"Come to Me, all of you who are weary and carry heavy burdens,
and I will give you rest."

MATT. 11:28

"Do not be afraid or discouraged,
for the Lord will personally go ahead of you."

Deut. 31:8

Those who live in the shelter of the Most High will find rest
in the shadow of the Almighty.

Ps. 91:1

Kind words are like honey – sweet to the soul and healthy for the body.

Prov. 16:24

"The joy of the LORD is your strength!"

NEH. 8:10

This is the day the LORD has made.
We will rejoice and be glad in it.

Ps. 118:24

Those who trust in the LORD will find new strength.
They will soar high on wings like eagles.

Isa. 40:31

"No eye has seen, no ear has heard, and no mind has imagined
what God has prepared for those who love Him."

1 Cor. 2:9

I will rejoice in the LORD! I will be joyful in the God of my salvation!

Nothing in all creation will ever be able to separate us from the love of God.

My health may fail, and my spirit may grow weak, but God remains
the strength of my heart; He is mine forever.

Ps. 73:26

See how very much our Father loves us, for He calls us
His children, and that is what we are!

1 John 3:1

"Blessed are all who hear the word of God
and put it into practice."

Luke 11:28

The Lord is my light and my salvation –
so why should I be afraid?

Ps. 27:1

"Be strong and courageous!
For the LORD your God is with you wherever you go."

JOSH. 1:9

He made us, and we are His. We are His people, the sheep of His pasture.

Ps. 100:3

Give your burdens to the LORD, and He will take care of you.

Ps. 55:22

Let God transform you into a new person by changing the way you think.

"Anything is possible if a person believes."

I can do everything through Christ, who gives me strength.

"Blessed are those who trust in the Lᴏʀᴅ and have made
the Lᴏʀᴅ their hope and confidence."

Jᴇʀ. 17:7

The Lord leads with unfailing love and faithfulness
all who keep His covenant and obey His demands.
Ps. 25:10

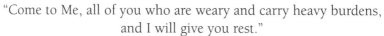

"Come to Me, all of you who are weary and carry heavy burdens,
and I will give you rest."

Matt. 11:28

"Do not be afraid or discouraged,
for the LORD will personally go ahead of you."

DEUT. 31:8

Those who live in the shelter of the Most High will find rest
in the shadow of the Almighty.

Ps. 91:1

"I will never fail you. I will never abandon you."

Heb. 13:5

Kind words are like honey – sweet to the soul and healthy for the body.

PROV. 16:24

"The joy of the Lord is your strength!"

Neh. 8:10

This is the day the LORD has made.
We will rejoice and be glad in it.

Ps. 118:24

Those who trust in the Lord will find new strength.
They will soar high on wings like eagles.
ISA. 40:31

"No eye has seen, no ear has heard, and no mind has imagined
what God has prepared for those who love Him."

1 Cor. 2:9

I will rejoice in the LORD! I will be joyful in the God of my salvation!

Nothing in all creation will ever be able to separate us from the love of God.

My health may fail, and my spirit may grow weak, but God remains
the strength of my heart; He is mine forever.

See how very much our Father loves us, for He calls us
His children, and that is what we are!

1 JOHN 3:1

"Blessed are all who hear the word of God
and put it into practice."

Luke 11:28

The Lord is my light and my salvation –
so why should I be afraid?

Ps. 27:1

"Be strong and courageous!
For the Lord your God is with you wherever you go."

Josh. 1:9

He made us, and we are His. We are His people, the sheep of His pasture.

Ps. 100:3

Give your burdens to the LORD, and He will take care of you.

Ps. 55:22

Let God transform you into a new person by changing the way you think.

<small>Rom. 12:2</small>

"God blesses those who work for peace,
for they will be called the children of God."

Matt. 5:9

"Anything is possible if a person believes."

MARK 9:23

I can do everything through Christ, who gives me strength.

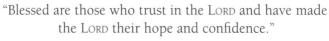

"Blessed are those who trust in the LORD and have made
the LORD their hope and confidence."

JER. 17:7

The LORD leads with unfailing love and faithfulness
all who keep His covenant and obey His demands.

Ps. 25:10

"Come to Me, all of you who are weary and carry heavy burdens, and I will give you rest."

Matt. 11:28

"Do not be afraid or discouraged,
for the Lord will personally go ahead of you."

Deut. 31:8

Those who live in the shelter of the Most High will find rest
in the shadow of the Almighty.

Ps. 91:1

"I will never fail you. I will never abandon you."

HEB. 13:5

Kind words are like honey – sweet to the soul and healthy for the body.

"The joy of the Lord is your strength!"

Neh. 8:10

This is the day the LORD has made.
We will rejoice and be glad in it.
Ps. 118:24

Those who trust in the Lord will find new strength.
They will soar high on wings like eagles.

"No eye has seen, no ear has heard, and no mind has imagined
what God has prepared for those who love Him."

1 Cor. 2:9

I will rejoice in the LORD! I will be joyful in the God of my salvation!

Nothing in all creation will ever be able to separate us from the love of God.

My health may fail, and my spirit may grow weak, but God remains
the strength of my heart; He is mine forever.

Ps. 73:26

See how very much our Father loves us, for He calls us
His children, and that is what we are!

1 John 3:1

"Blessed are all who hear the word of God
and put it into practice."

Luke 11:28

The Lord is my light and my salvation –
so why should I be afraid?

Ps. 27:1

"Be strong and courageous!
For the Lᴏʀᴅ your God is with you wherever you go."

Jᴏsʜ. 1:9

He made us, and we are His. We are His people, the sheep of His pasture.

Ps. 100:3

Give your burdens to the LORD, and He will take care of you.

Ps. 55:22

Let God transform you into a new person by changing the way you think.

Rom. 12:2

"God blesses those who work for peace,
for they will be called the children of God."

MATT. 5:9

"Anything is possible if a person believes."

I can do everything through Christ, who gives me strength.

"Blessed are those who trust in the LORD and have made
the LORD their hope and confidence."

JER. 17:7

The LORD leads with unfailing love and faithfulness
all who keep His covenant and obey His demands.

Ps. 25:10

"Come to Me, all of you who are weary and carry heavy burdens,
and I will give you rest."

Matt. 11:28

"Do not be afraid or discouraged,
for the Lᴏʀᴅ will personally go ahead of you."

Dᴇᴜᴛ. 31:8

Those who live in the shelter of the Most High will find rest
in the shadow of the Almighty.

Ps. 91:1

"I will never fail you. I will never abandon you."

Kind words are like honey – sweet to the soul and healthy for the body.

PROV. 16:24

"The joy of the Lord is your strength!"

Neh. 8:10

_____

This is the day the LORD has made.
We will rejoice and be glad in it.

PS. 118:24

Those who trust in the Lᴏʀᴅ will find new strength.
They will soar high on wings like eagles.

Isᴀ. 40:31

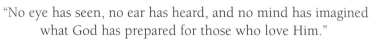

"No eye has seen, no ear has heard, and no mind has imagined
what God has prepared for those who love Him."

1 Cor. 2:9

I will rejoice in the Lord! I will be joyful in the God of my salvation!

Hab. 3:18

Nothing in all creation will ever be able to separate us from the love of God.

My health may fail, and my spirit may grow weak, but God remains
the strength of my heart; He is mine forever.

Ps. 73:26

See how very much our Father loves us, for He calls us
His children, and that is what we are!

1 John 3:1

"Blessed are all who hear the word of God
and put it into practice."

Luke 11:28

The Lord is my light and my salvation –
so why should I be afraid?

"Be strong and courageous!
For the Lord your God is with you wherever you go."

Josh. 1:9

He made us, and we are His. We are His people, the sheep of His pasture.

Ps. 100:3

Give your burdens to the LORD, and He will take care of you.

Ps. 55:22

Let God transform you into a new person by changing the way you think.

"God blesses those who work for peace,
for they will be called the children of God."

MATT. 5:9

"Anything is possible if a person believes."

MARK 9:23

I can do everything through Christ, who gives me strength.

"Blessed are those who trust in the Lᴏʀᴅ and have made
the Lᴏʀᴅ their hope and confidence."

Jᴇʀ. 17:7

The LORD leads with unfailing love and faithfulness
all who keep His covenant and obey His demands.

Ps. 25:10

"Come to Me, all of you who are weary and carry heavy burdens,
and I will give you rest."

MATT. 11:28

"Do not be afraid or discouraged,
for the Lord will personally go ahead of you."

Deut. 31:8

Those who live in the shelter of the Most High will find rest
in the shadow of the Almighty.

Ps. 91:1

"I will never fail you. I will never abandon you."

HEB. 13:5

Kind words are like honey – sweet to the soul and healthy for the body.

PROV. 16:24

"The joy of the Lord is your strength!"

Neh. 8:10

This is the day the LORD has made.
We will rejoice and be glad in it.

Ps. 118:24

Those who trust in the LORD will find new strength.
They will soar high on wings like eagles.

ISA. 40:31

"No eye has seen, no ear has heard, and no mind has imagined
what God has prepared for those who love Him."

1 Cor. 2:9

I will rejoice in the LORD! I will be joyful in the God of my salvation!

HAB. 3:18

Nothing in all creation will ever be able to separate us from the love of God.

My health may fail, and my spirit may grow weak, but God remains
the strength of my heart; He is mine forever.

Ps. 73:26

See how very much our Father loves us, for He calls us
His children, and that is what we are!

1 JOHN 3:1